A LIVING LEGEND

Born in a broom cupboard, brought up in grinding poverty in the sewers of King's Cross, how did Roland Rat become a superstar — a legend in his own lifetime?

At last, the authorised life story — a saga that goes deep below the surface and embraces three generations of the Rat family of King's Cross, and their historic struggles against the grasping perfumed-mustachioed de Farceys.

A thrilling drama of showbiz and heartache, of a family seeking fulfilment, set against a background of the London Blitz and the glittering lights of Sunday Night at the London Palladium. And the final triumph of Roland Rat, Superstar, keeping faith with destiny.

Roland Rat

A LIVING LEGEND

The authorised life story
of a rodent of substance

ANNE DIGBY

Hippo Books
Scholastic Publications Limited
London

To David, Roland's closest friend

Scholastic Publications Ltd.,
10 Earlham Street, London WC2H 9RX, UK

Scholastic Inc.,
730 Broadway, New York, NY 10003, USA

Scholastic Tab Publications Ltd.,
123 Newkirk Road, Richmond Hill,
Ontario L4C 3G5, Canada

Ashton Scholastic Pty. Ltd.,
PO Box 579, Gosford, New South Wales,
Australia

Ashton Scholastic Ltd.,
165 Marua Road, Panmure, Auckland 6,
New Zealand

First published by Scholastic Publications Limited, 1987

ISBN 0 590 70582 2

Made and printed by Cox and Wyman, Berks
Typeset in Plantin by AKM Associates (UK) Ltd.,
Ajmal House, Hayes Road, Southall, London

CONTENTS

ROLAND
RAT

Acknowledgements

It was in 1983 that Roland, realizing that he had become a superstar, contacted me with a view to my writing the authorised life story. It was such an honour that I knew this would be the greatest challenge of my writing career.

Obviously there was an amazing story here. To come from the squalid background of a family that for generations had known only grinding poverty and humiliation and to find yourself, within a few short weeks, a living legend had to be a truly remarkable achievement. Especially for a rat. Would I be able to do justice to such a story?

Now after three years of painstaking research and ferreting around, I can at last present the work that Ratfans have been waiting for. Here is the authentic life story, revealing the amazing facts — many of them previously unknown even to Roland himself — for the very first time.

A priori I would like to express my indebtedness to older generations of the Rat family who have given unstintingly of their time and reminiscences and have allowed me complete freedom of access to all the family's private papers. I thank especially Roland's parents, Iris and Freddy, without whom this story could never have been told.

For information about the wicked de Farcey family I am grateful for data supplied by the

Italian Ice Cream Traders' Association; the Association of British Travel Agents; the National Society of Secondhand Car Dealers; the Society of Theatrical Agents; the Association of Computer Dating Agencies and the Office of Fair Trading. All of it is disreputable.

I would also like to thank London Transport for allowing me to camp on Platform 3 (northbound) at King's Cross station while conducting important interviews; Glenis and Kevin for typing the manuscript; and above all Roland himself for giving me twenty minutes of his time free of charge and supplying the typewriter ribbons.

I dedicate this book to them all — and to Ratfans everywhere.

ANNE DIGBY
Cap d'Antibes 1986

Chapter One

A DATE WITH DESTINY

Victor is a very old and frail rodent now. His sight is weak and he has arthritis from years and years of living in damp sewers. He walks very slowly with the aid of two sticks.

But there is pride in the old rat's quavering voice as he shows visitors around his beautiful little sewer in North London, *Mon Repos*. His retirement home — situated at Hendon on the Northern Line — was bought for him by his grandson Roland. It is equipped with every luxury that money can buy. In pride of place, obscuring an original Woolworths Renoir on the wall, is a colour TV with a screen of stupendous size.

"Never miss him on the TV, I don't," says old Victor. Victor has a private masseur who comes in daily from Amersham, as well as a home help hedgehog who cooks for him.

"A bit prickly she is. But she's a good cook. The missus passed away a long time ago." He wipes a tear from his eye. "Caught pneumonia in the bad winter of '78. She went to fetch a lump of coal that'd dropped off a lorry in the Caledonian Road, and struggled all the way back to the sewer in the icy wind. It was so heavy, and she was so exhausted, she slipped in the sludge and got chilled to the bones. She was never strong, the missus. We had a hard life, yer know. That bunch of dirty de Farceys have got a lot to answer for," he adds. He tends to refer to the de Farcey family in the terms that some misguided humans reserve for rats.

Victor sinks down into the comfort of his quilted armchair and warms himself in front of the fire for a while, silent with his memories.

Then — that note of pride again.

"Our Roly pays for everything, yer know. He offered to build me a granddad annexe next to the Ratcave, that flashy place he's had built under King's Cross underground station, but London ain't the place it used to be. In my young day you could get the last tube back from the Elephant & Castle without a care in the world. Had it all to yourself and the worst thing that could happen was to get yer tail caught in the sliding doors. But not no more. Oh, yeah, Roly's looked after me since he got to be a superstar. Just like he's looked after Iris and Freddy. Roly's seen us all right."

More silence. Then Victor says, modestly:

"I like to think Roly's inherited his talent from me. Mind you Freddy will say it's from him, but then Freddy got his talent from me in the first place. Us Rats have always had showbiz in our blood but it's been nothing but setbacks and heartbreak till our Roly made it. He did it! He had the guts to make the big breakthrough! We had a date with destiny, us Rats — and Roly was the one to keep it."

So the story of Roland Rat, living legend, by rights begins nearly half a century ago.

Chapter Two

ENTER THE DE FARCEYS

It was the terrible winter of 1940 and the height of the London Blitz! The Allied Forces had been forced to retreat from Dunkirk. Italy had entered the war and Mussolini's troops had overrun the south of France. From Berlin, Goering had given orders that London be bombed into submission.

In their basement flat in the Farringdon Road, the de Farcey brothers cowered in fear.

They were frightened of the bombs, of course, but there was more to it than that.

The family name had not been de Farcey for very long. It had until recently been *da Farci.*

The three brothers were Italian. They had fled from their native land in the 1930s, following an unfortunate incident concerning some rotten fish.

This was on the occasion of Benito Mussolini's one and only visit to Sicily. The mayor had decided that no expense should be spared. He ordered that a lavish banquet be prepared for *Il Duce* and the da Farci brothers landed the lucrative catering contract for this big occasion. Pleased to locate a cheap box of fish that had been left on the quayside in the hot sun a little too long, they dressed it up with sauces and garnishes for the banquet.

Unfortunately, after dinner, *Il Duce*, strutting and posturing on the platform that had been erected in the town's main piazza, was violently sick in the middle of his big speech. In the direct line of fire on the platform was a dark stranger wearing diamond rings and a very expensive new suit. The suit, which had been especially made for the occasion in Rome, was ruined.

The excitement roused the audience, and there was much clapping and cheering and stamping of feet in the piazza. But the brow of the stranger knitted and his face went dark like his suit.

That night he said to the local Mafia (for he was the Godfather, no less), "Find out who did the catering. And when you have found them . . ."

He ran his forefinger from his left ear, down under his chin and up to his right ear.

"*Basta!*" he added, which is Italian for "It suffices" or "That's quite enough of that."

But the da Farci brothers had already fled. With all their worldly possessions in three suitcases they had boarded the P & O liner anchored in the bay and were now heading for England. For the next few days they listened to lectures on "The Italian Experience: Art Treasures of the Mediterranean", went to tea dances in the afternoons, and counted their blessings frequently at their narrow escape from certain death.

Benito Mussolini never visited Sicily again.

The da Farci brothers adapted to life in England quickly. They settled in central London and embarked upon various business ventures until they found the one that suited them.

They sold imitation Italian ice cream from barrows outside London tube stations. They ran this business successfully for two years, although sometimes it involved quite a lot of running. Then came the war.

They quickly changed their names by deed poll from *da Farci* to the French-sounding *de Farcey*. They painted the new name on their ice cream barrows and changed the words "Genuine Italian Ice Cream" to "Genuine French Ice Cream".

Throughout 1940 they posed as heroes of the French resistance, forced to flee to England from the Nazis.

"We only sell ice cream as cover," Antonio de Farcey, the eldest brother, would tell the customers. "We are members of the Free French Army, doing secret underground work in Londra — scusi Londres."

But now they were frightened. All over England, Italians were being interned.

It was London's darkest hour. The population was feeling intensely patriotic. Londoners were beginning to look askance at the de Farcey brothers with their heavily perfumed dark curly mustaches and swarthy complexions. *French* ice cream?

"People are getting suspicious," said Antonio.

Only that afternoon, he had sold some ice cream to a wounded soldier back from Dunkirk. The Tommy had tasted it, thrown it in his face in disgust and said, "You don't look blinkin' French to me."

'We can't go on like this," said Antonio.

His brothers agreed. They decided to put the ice cream business into cold storage for the duration of the war, took scissors in hand and hacked their beautiful long mustachios down to size. The size, in fact, that Antonio's great-nephew, the well-known Darcey de Farcey, wears to this day.

"Now I *will* pass for a Frenchman," said Antonio. "And from now on I shall call myself 'Anton' for short. You two can do what you like, but I think I have found a brilliant new career."

"What's that?"

Anton smiled and tried to twirl his long mustachios until he realized they were lying on the floor. He dabbed a little perfume on the remnants left on his upper lip.

"Last night, down in King's Cross tube

station, I witnessed something remarkable. A rat with a voice like Caruso! And everybody refused to believe me. But imagine it! Such talent cannot be wasted! Oh, no. It *must* not be wasted. It *will* not be wasted!"

He rubbed his hands together with glee.

"Brothers," he announced. "I am going into show business. I shall have cards printed at once:

ANTON DE FARCEY
THEATRICAL AGENT."

He threw back his head and roared with laughter, showing the gleaming gold fillings in his teeth.

"This is where I go underground," he giggled.

Chapter Three

A YOUNG RAT OF AMBITION

Along with thousands of other hopeful young rodents, Victor came to Central London to look for work.

He set off from the Isle of Dogs in 1939 wearing a serge suit and cloth cap. Some food for the journey was wrapped in a spotted kerchief, slung from a stick over his shoulder.

"There are no jobs for you here, Victor," his mother said tearfully, as she held him close in a last fond embrace. "Don't forget to write. And keep singing. You've got a lovely voice, son."

"I'm *going* to be a singer, mum! As soon as I get a job I'm going to pay for some singing lessons."

Alas for the dreams of youth.

Victor moved in with an uncle at King's Cross and tramped the sewers of London for weeks in search of work. Then came the big break. London Transport were planning to extend the Northern line to Elstree and Borehamwood. The work was due to start at last and a sub-contractor was recruiting rats to help with a new tunnel. Victor was taken on.

"Uncle! Uncle!" he shouted in excitement when he came home with the news. "I've got a job! I start on Monday."

But when he reported for work he was given his cards.

"Sorry, son. We've just declared war on Hitler," he was told. "Every penny's needed for the war effort now. London Transport's had to cancel the project until further notice."

After that, every door seemed to be closed to Victor. He volunteered for the army but was turned down because he was too short. None of the munitions factories wanted him. In fact there were huge posters on every hoarding saying he was a pest. For rats, emboldened by hunger, had started to make a nuisance of themselves.

He was one of a vast army of unemployed rodents.

The big sewer directly under King's Cross underground station was densely overpopulated in those days: an inner city slum. The rather grand rat holes that had been built in the prosperous years after the First World War, when a rat could make his fortune helping to build the London Underground, were now seedy and run down. They had been divided and subdivided as rats poured in from Jarrow and other places in the north and midlands.

Victor eked out a living by collecting whelks in the early hours of a Sunday. These were often dropped on the platform late on a Saturday night after people had been to the pub. He sold them from a little cart in the sewer every Sunday morning.

He was determined to keep cheerful.

His ambition to be a singer burned as brightly as ever. With times as bad as they were he needed his dream to keep him going. Besides, he had fallen in love with Winifred, a lovely young rat who lived at the Elephant & Castle. One day, he vowed, when he had found fame and fortune in showbiz, they would get married and raise a family. He would buy Winnie a beautiful home somewhere in the country maybe, or Hendon. . . .

He listened to the popular songs on the wireless and learned them off by heart. Some of the old rats in the sewer loved it when he came round and sang to them on a Sunday evening. Victor idolised Bing Crosby and his imitation of Bing singing "I'm Dreaming of a White Christmas" would bring tears to their eyes.

Then, one weekend in 1940, Victor got a terrible shock.

It was very early on Sunday morning.

Victor, as always, ventured out of his lodgings, knotted kerchief over his shoulder, to embark on his weekly whelk-collecting expedition. A run from the sewer led directly up to the tracks where the Northern line trains ran.

He loved King's Cross tube station at this time of night. It was always silent and still. The last trains to Edgware and High Barnet and Mill Hill East and Morden had long since rattled through. The live rail was switched off.

He followed a simple routine. First he walked up and down the tracks, eyes skinned for squashed whelks. Once he had combed the tracks, he would clamber up on to the platforms and work his way along them from end to end. By dawn his kerchief was invariably crammed full of whelks for his barrow, and sometimes a few roast chestnuts as well.

And as he worked, he sang.

That was what he liked best of all. To have the whole tube tunnel to himself, with its marvellous acoustics. To let rip in a way he dare not in the overcrowded slums down below. It gave him a chance to indulge in his new-found love of opera, picked up from his uncle's wireless. Puccini was his latest craze.

On the night in question, he emerged from the run into the tube tunnel and jumped up on to one of the silver rails. With eyes closed he pretended he was in the Covent Garden Opera House or at La Scala in Milan. He placed a hand on his chest and began to sing at the top of his voice:

"*Your tiny hand is frozen. Let me warm it into life. . .*"

Then — "*Mama mia!*"

Victor opened his eyes. Who was that? He felt scared. Craning his neck and gazing upwards, he saw the towering figure of a man standing at the edge of the platform and staring straight down at him. He had brown eyes and a long curly mustache. He wore a white overall with *De Farcey's Genuine French Ice Cream* embroidered on it.

Then the man started to shout with excitement. Victor got the impression that there were other people behind him, but the platform was too high up for him to be able to see.

"There's a rat down here!" the man was crying. "And 'e's singing. He sings just like Caruso!"

Panic-stricken, Victor heard a babble of voices all along the platform.

"Shurrup you twerp. We're trying to get to sleep."

"Been drinkin', this bloke?"

"Get him out of here. Me missus is trying to get to sleep!"

Scuffling broke out, and Victor caught a glimpse of the man being dragged away from the edge of the platform, still protesting,

"A rat, I tell you! Singing!"

But he didn't wait to see any more.

Terrified, he turned tail and fled, back down the run to the safety of the sewer. As he tip-toed back into his lodgings, his heart was going pit-pat, pit-pat.

He hung his empty kerchief up, climbed into bed and hid under the blankets, feeling miserable.

The tube station had been overrun by humans.

On the following day, a wise old rat in Victor's sewer explained to him what was going on.

"It's the Blitz, son," he explained. "The bombs is falling thick and fast up top. So Winston Churchill's said that all Londoners can come down and sleep in the tubes every night, if they wants to."

"But what about the whelks?" asked Victor in despair.

"You can still collect yer whelks, son, if you can find them. Just keep yer head down, that's all. Creep about as quiet as a mouse. Don't draw no attention to yourself. Most of them humans'll be fast asleep, bless 'em, the rotten time they're having of it. Go on, son. Next weekend, you give it a try."

As the whelks were Victor's only means of livelihood, he didn't have much choice.

The following weekend, at two in the morning, he screwed up his courage and went back up.

He tip-toed along the tracks, collecting squashed whelks. He gave a nervous little start every time he heard a noise. There must be hundreds of people up there on the platform, judging by the grunts and whistles and snores. He was going to miss his singing practice. Badly. But as long as he didn't sing, with a bit of luck nobody would notice him. . . .

"*Pssst!*"

Victor jumped. He'd just reached the end of the tracks, where they disappeared into the tube tunnel. A man was standing in the shadows of the tunnel, beckoning to him.

"Don't be scared," the man whispered. "Come here."

Heart thumping, Victor ventured into the tunnel. The man bent down to speak to him. Suddenly Victor realized it was the man with the long mustache, except now the mustache was very short, and he wasn't wearing the white overall any more. The man handed him a card. He said, "Can you read what this says? It says: 'ANTON DE FARCEY — THEATRICAL AGENT' "

Then, as if in a dream, Victor heard the words he'd always longed to hear.

"Want to know something? I'm going to make you a star."

Chapter Four

THE END OF THE DREAM

Victor blinked. A real live theatrical agent in the tube tunnel? And he was whispering amazing, wonderful things — "From the moment I hear you sing, I know you have great talent. I know I can make you a star. Every night for a week I come down here, searching, searching. I — the great Anton de Farcey. Hoping to see you again! Hoping you will sign up with me and let me be your agent."

Those thrilling, magical words whirled round and round in Victor's brain. Were they really meant for him? Surely the man must have made a mistake?

Victor looked round just in case there were somebody standing behind him. But — no. The two of them were all alone.

"You really mean me, mister?"

"Sure I do. See my address — on my card?"

"Er?" asked Victor.

"You're holding it upside down. Can't you read?"

Shamefaced, Victor hung his head.

"I can't read nor write. I never went to school, see."

"All the better!" said Anton de Farcey. "Schools are terrible places. Your talent would have been crushed. You don't need to be able to read and write. You've got me to look after your interests now. So. I tell you where my office is and you memorize it. Then you come and see me nine o'clock on Monday morning. I will have contract, all ready for you to sign."

"Th-thank you. Oh, thank you," stuttered Victor. He was completely overcome with emotion. "I'll be there, mister, I mean, sir. Are you foreign, sir?"

"Si! Je suis French!" replied Anton with a smooth smile. "As well as being a theatrical agent I am doing secret work for the Free French army and de Gaulle. But you have never heard of me? I am called Monsieur Showbiz in France. Have you heard of Maurice Chevalier — ?"

Victor nodded eagerly.

"I discovered him." Anton examined his fingernails and blew nonchalantly on them. "And the Folies Bergères?"

"Yes!"

"*My* idea," said Anton. "Good, huh?"

"You bet!" said Victor. "And you think you can make me a star? Oohh." (*99, Farringdon Road . . . 99, Farringdon Road. . . .* Victor kept reciting the address in his brain.)

"*Absolument.*" Anton glanced up from the tunnel to the rows of sleeping Londoners on the platform. Some of them were beginning to stir.

"Who's that twerp talking to himself in the tunnel?"

"Shurrup can't you? We're trying to sleep."

Anton de Farcey bent and whispered in Victor's ear, "Nine o'clock Monday morning then. At my office. Don't be late!"

"I won't, Mr de Farcey," said Victor.

The next few months were the happiest Victor had ever known.

He signed the contract with Anton de Farcey, marking it with a cross.

"I have seen too many young stars ruined by sudden wealth," Mr de Farcey then explained to him. For that reason he said he would take sole charge of finance, placing all Victor's earnings in a big money box. It would be there waiting for him at the end of the Blitz. He would also get a small weekly allowance.

There was no need to book a theatre; they were going on tour. They would appear nightly on tube platforms all over London, keeping up everybody's spirits during the dark days of the Blitz.

"Victor, you will sing all the favourites. Sad songs, happy songs," his agent told him. "We will appear nightly at ten o'clock, as the people are settling down for the night. They will get ready to go to sleep with lovely music ringing in their ears."

Victor had just one big worry.

"And it won't matter, me being a rat?"

"If you were on your own, *yes!*" said his agent. "They would never accept you. The world is not ready. But with me by your side, Victor, you will be all right. You will stand on my right shoulder as you sing — and then they will accept you."

So they appeared nightly on all the top West End platforms. Leicester Square, the Strand and Charing Cross on the Northern line, Piccadilly Circus and Green Park on the Piccadilly line, and Trafalgar Square on the Bakerloo.

White Christmas. . . . Somewhere Over the Rainbow. . . . Tosca. . . . My Very Good Friend, the Milkman. . . .

Perched on Anton's shoulder, Victor sang his heart out. The people of London wept with emotion. The coins cascaded into Anton's trilby hat.

Victor felt fulfilled as a singer. It was wonderful to be in showbiz — to be in full-time work. Anton allowed him 1/9½d a week, which is about 9 pence in today's money. But it wasn't the money that made Victor's heart swell with pride. It was the knowledge that he was helping Londoners get through the dark days of the

Blitz! In his own small, patriotic way, he was helping Britain's war effort.

Sometimes Victor felt a pang of envy at the way Anton got all the recognition. It was always Anton who got his hand shaken. It was always Anton who had to sign the autographs.

"You see, you cannot read or write," explained his agent. "I have to sign your name for you."

Victor never dreamed that he was being tricked. He never realized as he stood on Anton's shoulder, singing his heart out, that Anton was miming all the words of the songs.

The people of London thought that Anton de Farcey was the great singer, not Victor at all. They smiled to themselves at the pet rat who went everywhere with his master — the little mascot who opened and closed his mouth as his master sang.

It was Anton de Farcey's name that was scribbled on all the *Evening Stars* and *Standards* — not Victor's.

But Victor never suspected any of this. It was a blissful period of his life. It was not until he married Winifred at the end of the London Blitz, that the great blow fell.

The bombing of London was over and people were no longer sleeping every night on the tube platforms. The deep stations had made excellent shelters during the Blitz, but now everyone could sleep peacefully in their own beds again. Victor's contract was due to be renewed. He went to Anton de Farcey's office to collect his money, as promised.

"Please can I have me cash now, Mr de Farcey?" he asked timidly, eyeing the large metal cash box on his agent's desk.

Thrilled to have made it in showbiz, or so he thought, Victor had recently married Winnie and they were living in his uncle's lodging house in the sewer, waiting for the great moment when Victor received his lump sum from Mr de Farcey. Then they would buy a place of their own! For two weeks now they had been house-hunting, looking at lovely places in the country — Chesham Bois, Ponders End, Cockfosters. Winifred had been planning all the furniture she would buy.

"Certainly, Victor."

Anton de Farcey unlocked the cash box with a big key and poured a heap of coins on to the desk. Then he counted them and put them into three piles.

"There we are, Victor," he said, pushing the piles across the table. "This is all yours. After expenses. Four pounds, sixteen shillings and fourpence-halfpenny."

Victor felt faint all over with shock and disappointment.

"£4/16/4½d?" he said. "Is that all? What expenses?"

The agent fished out of a drawer the contract Victor had signed.

"Look, bambino, it's all written down here. Agent's commission 75 per cent of gross earnings. Advertising and incidental expenses: 3½ per cent. Withholding tax against Inland Revenue demands: 21 per cent. But the rest is yours."

Victor shovelled the coins into his pocket sadly. In a small voice, he asked "What about a new contract then, Mr de Farcey?"

He had to stay in showbiz! He couldn't be unemployed again, for Winnie's sake. "You said you'd give me a new contract after this one, if me act was a success. You said you'd give me an increase. Well, the act *has* been a success. . . ."

"Not a big enough success," de Farcey cut in. He dabbed a little perfume on his mustache then examined his fingernails. "I am going to Scotland tomorrow. There is singer up there called Harry Lauder. He ask me to be agent. *Mi scusa*, now. I am very busy man."

As Victor left the room, head bowed, de Farcey called out:

"You can always try to be a big star on your own."

Egged on by Winifred, Victor *did* try. Just once. The very next day, quaking with nerves, he approached a long line of ladies queueing for bread near King's Cross Station. He opened his mouth to sing and a nervous high note came out. And suddenly ladies in hair curlers and turbans were yelling at him and throwing things and telling him to go away.

He slunk home in black despair. . . .

"I've let yer down, love," he told Winnie. "I feel like jumping off the side of the sewer."

"Not sewer-side, Victor! Not that!" cried Winifred, holding him close. "We'll manage somehow, I know we will. We love each other, don't we?"

And somehow they did manage.

But Victor never ventured into showbiz again.

It was just as Anton de Farcey had told him in the first place. The world was not yet ready to welcome a Rat as a superstar. That historic moment was more than forty years away.

But for Victor, it was the end of the dream.

Chapter Five

FREDDY AND IRIS

Eventually Victor got a job in the building trade. Winifred was taking in washing, so they were able to scrimp and save until they had enough money to set up home on their own, away from King's Cross.

They handed over their savings as key money in return for a tiny little flat under a loose floorboard in a dressing room at the London Palladium.

"We've been ripped off, Victor," said Winnie, on the day they moved in, though she was thrilled to have a place of her own at last.

"We're right in the heart of theatreland," said Victor. "And that's all that matters. We'll be able to smell the greasepaint and hear the stars walking about, just over our heads. Imagine it!"

Victor knew that this was the closest he would ever get to showbiz now. His failed career had left a deep wound. He rarely talked about his days as a singer on the West End platforms of London, not even to Winifred.

"Oh, Victor!" Tears of emotion welled up into Winifred's eyes. "I ain't ever heard you say anything about showbiz since. . . . since. . . ." Now she understood why he'd set his heart on this hole. She walked over and kissed him. "It's smashing here, Vic. Really smashing. I know we're going to be happy."

"Well, it's a showbiz address, love," said Victor gruffly, "London W.1. It may be an 'umble 'ome, but it's where I belong."

So it came about that their son Freddy — father of Roland Rat, superstar — was born under a dressing room in the London Palladium. Born to the smell of greasepaint. And thus the Rat family moved inexorably one step further along the road toward their destiny.

Freddy was a lively, adventurous little rat, always into mischief, and the apple of his father's eye.

Now the war was over, London's theatres were ablaze with light and spangled with colour.

Once in his teens, there was nothing Freddy

liked better than to slip out of his room at night and ride on the roof of a double-decker bus around the West End. He would blink up at the names of the stars, written in twinkling lights. Sometimes he would mingle with the theatre-going crowds, drinking in the atmosphere.

He liked it best when a famous star was using the upstairs dressing room at home. Ear pressed to the floorboard, he would listen to them walking about overhead. Sometimes they would be practising funny lines, other times singing a few bars of a hit song.

Once they were out on stage, he would prise up the loose floorboard and scamper around looking for souvenirs.

His room was crammed to bursting point with showbiz memorabilia. By his bed was a piece of the carpet that Frank Sinatra had stood on. On a shelf were the cigarette ends of the famous, each carefully labelled by name: *Billie Holliday*, *Elvis Presley*[1], *The Everley Brothers* (two), and many others.

The walls were plastered with old theatre programmes. In pride of place on the mantel-

[1] *The authenticity of this has been questioned in a recent paper published by Dr. Lisa Lott, professor of show business memorabilia at Wapping Polytechnic. She claims that the only genuine Elvis Presley cigarette stub extant in England was found at London airport on the one occasion that Presley visited the U.K. and that he never appeared at the London Palladium. Freddy has always maintained that Presley did walk past the stage door of the Palladium on that one visit and threw down the stub. It may have been a Presley lookalike.* *See biographer's note (2) on p. 82.*

piece was an empty coke bottle that Tommy Steele had drunk from and a comb that Cliff Richard had carelessly left behind.

Freddy idolised both Frank Sinatra and Cliff Richard. He knew most of their hit songs by heart and would often sing them.

"You've got talent, son," his father told him. "Just like me. Just like I used to have."

"I want to be in showbiz, Dad."

"Don't try and be a star, son. Look what happened to me. I wanted too much, too soon. That just leads to heartbreak and bitterness. Try and get a job backstage. That way you won't get hurt."

Freddy had his dreams, but he had the sense to keep them to himself.

"I'll take any job that comes," vowed Freddy, "as long as it's in showbiz! I've got to make the right contacts, that's what."

Freddy took to hanging around the pub next door to the London Palladium at nights, in the hope of meeting somebody influential. After many months his patience was rewarded.

"Hey, you," said a dark-haired young man one night. "Aren't you Victor's son?"

It was closing time and the pub was emptying. The man had put his foot out and stopped Freddy at the door.

'That's right," said Freddy in surprise.

"My Dad knew your Dad, way back in the war. He's often told me about him."

"What's your name then?"

"Mick de Farcey," he replied, smoothing his mustache.

It was true. Anton de Farcey had met and

married a pretty Irish girl during the war, in order to get an Irish passport. Mick was their younger son. Darcey de Farcey's famous Uncle Mick.

"Your Dad swindled my Dad," said Freddy suspiciously.

"I know," said Mick. "And I've been wanting to make it up to your family ever since. How would you like a job in showbiz? A nice steady job?"

"Like it? Cor!" said Freddy.

"Listen here, then." He took Freddy into a dark corner of the bar and produced a contract. "There's going to be a fantastic TV show starting next Sunday. It's to be called 'Sunday Night at the London Palladium', and it's going out live every week. Bruce Forsyth is going to be the compère, introducing all the top stars who come on his show. He's good. This show's going to run for years and years, I tell you."

"Where do I come in?" asked Freddy. He tried not to reveal his excitement.

"Simple," said Mick. "This new show's all about razzmatazz and glamour and glitter. The swinging sixties! It's going to have a shimmering stage that goes round and round. That's where you come in. You help push it."

"Oh!" said Freddy.

"Fancy it? Because if you don't, I've got plenty more rats to interview."

"It — it's a job," said Freddy. "I was *looking* for a job in showbiz. Are there prospects?"

"Sure," said Mick. "Back stage today — front stage tomorrow. That's show business. Are you on?"

Freddy nodded.

"Just sign here. First dress rehearsal tomorrow, six o'clock. £1 a week to start with, less my commission. Money for jam. Okay?"

"Done," said Freddy.

It was hardly a glamorous job. Even Freddy realized that. He was one of a team of thirty rats on a treadmill beneath the stage at the London Palladium. By running on the treads non-stop they were able to turn the revolving stage above to order. It was gruelling work. There were several rehearsals each week, as well as the live show on Sunday night.

But at least he was in showbiz. The theatre had always been in his blood, and now he was closer to the stars than ever. Once he heard one of the Beatles belch!

And like his father before him, he had his dreams.

Perhaps one day *he* would be up there on that revolving stage. A star. . . .

A romantic dreamer, Freddy. Handsome with it, too.

Someone was bound to fall hopelessly in love with him, sooner or later.

And when a sweet, rather plain rat called Iris met him at a party, she did.

Chapter Six

TO SEEK A BETTER LIFE

Iris pursued Freddy relentlessly. She wrote to him every day. She would even wait with her knitting outside the theatre in the hope of catching a glimpse of him. Coming from a stolid and respectable Euston family, Freddy Rat had brought the romance of the theatre into her dull life.

Soon Freddy was as much in love with Iris as she was with him. What she lacked in brains and beauty she made up for in character. She was loyal, dependable, and (what really mattered) told everyone he was wonderful.

She was so excited to have a boyfriend in showbiz!

But her parents were less impressed.

They lived in comfort directly beneath a weighing machine standing halfway along the Northern line platform at Euston.

The machine was faulty. Sometimes the pennies went where they were supposed to. But at other times they clonked down inside the weighing machine and fell through a large crack in the station platform. This crack was just above the front door of the family home and provided them with a very comfortable income.

"Pennies from heaven," Iris's father called them.

They had built up a large nest-egg of money. And some of it was earmarked for Iris. It would be her dowry.

"It'll be a lucky rat who marries our Iris," her father was fond of saying to his wife. "She's no beauty, but with the dowry we're going to give her, they'll start married life very comfortably."

"And *we'll* have a big say in who she marries," Iris's mother would reply smugly. "She'll have a lovely wedding with six bridesmaids and a huge cake, but she won't marry any old Tom, Dick or Harry. Oh dear me, no. She needs somebody sensible, with a good career and good prospects. Only the best will be good enough for our Iris."

And that didn't include Freddy.

"What a scruffy-looking, dreamy-faced good-for-nothing!" complained her mother, when Iris brought Freddy home for the first time. "Whatever do you see in *him?*"

"Freddy's wonderful!" Iris blubbed. "He's talented! He's in showbiz! He's got a wonderful voice and one day he's going to be — to be a star! What's more —" with a shriek and a sob, "I *LOVE* him!"

A stamping of feet and slamming of doors followed as she flounced off and locked herself in her bedroom.

It was a whirlwind courtship. The sixties were at their most swinging. On his nights off Freddy would take Iris to the theatre, backstage. They saw all the best shows. Afterwards they would eat at Maxim's, or the Astor Club, going in the back way of course.

But at other times, when they were flat broke, they were equally happy just being together. They would walk hand in hand through the streets of London, looking at the lights. And then they would go back to Freddy's place. Iris loved those times under the dressing room at the Palladium; having a laugh and a joke with Freddy's Mum and Dad; eating the squashed chips that she and Freddy had collected on their West End walkabouts. Best of all she liked looking at Freddy's show business collection.

"A bead from Lily Langtry's necklace! You *sure*, Freddy?"

"I swear it. A very old rat gave it to me last week."

One day he pressed something in her paw to be her very own. Elvis Presley's cigarette stub!

"Oh, *Freddy*. It means so much to you."

"*Garn.* Not so much as Frank Sinatra's carpet," said Freddy. He ran into his room, stood on the carpet and sang, just as his idol did: "*They can't take that away from me. . . .*"

The two of them looked at each other and laughed and laughed. It was such fun, just being together. They were hopelessly, helplessly in love. Suddenly serious, Freddy took Iris by the hand.

"Will you marry me, Iris? I love you passionate."

"Yes, Freddy. Oh, yes!"

But Iris was under age and needed her parents' consent.

"No, no, a thousand times no," said her father. "He's not good enough for you. He's just a starstruck dreamer with no prospects."

That night Iris and Freddy met in secret and decided to elope.

"There's a place where they marry you. It's called something Green," she said.

Freddy stared at a map of the London underground.

"There it is. Golders Green."

"There . . . there won't be any dowry now, Freddy," said Iris sadly. "We needed that money. It could have helped put you on the road to fame and fortune."

Freddy took her in his arms, in a fond embrace.

"I don't want no dowry, Iris. I love you for yourself. Besides, we'll be keeping Elvis Presley's cigarette stub in the family now."

And so the romantic young lovers eloped to Golders Green and got married, and Iris was cut off without a penny from the weighing machine.

Freddy's great-uncle found the newly-weds a little place of their own in his sewer at King's Cross. From now on Freddy had to commute to his job at the London Palladium. Bit by bit he brought all his precious things back to King's Cross after work. Frank Sinatra's carpet, Tommy Steele's coke bottle, all the old theatre programmes. . . .

"Now it feels like home," he told Iris.

"It is very damp down here," said Iris, shivering. "We *will* have enough money for fuel this winter, won't we, Freddy?"

" 'Course we will. That's why we didn't have no honeymoon, to pay for the fuel."

"We will have a honeymoon one day, won't we, Freddy? When you're a star?"

" 'Course, my love. One day when we're stinkin' rich, we'll have a honeymoon."

They were very happy at first. But it was a life of grinding poverty. Times were hard. Iris had to take in sewing. After a while she began to nag, just a little. She'd been used to better things.

"Why don't you ask that Mick de Farcey to give you a rise?"

"He won't."

"When are you going to get off that treadmill, Freddy? You'll never be a star if you carry on like this."

Freddy made no reply. A feeling of helplessness was beginning to seep over him, as it had his father before him.

"I never seem to get no lucky breaks, Iris."

"Freddy."

"Yes?"

"Freddy, I want to ask you something. If we ever have a baby, will you promise me one thing?"

"What?"

"Can I have it in hospital? My cousin Flora's just had a baby. She had it in hospital. Oh, Freddy, I'd like to have my baby in hospital!"

" 'Course you can," Freddy said gruffly. He took her by the hand. "If you ever have a baby, you'll have it in hospital. Cross my heart."

Secretly Freddy decided that they couldn't afford to have a baby, anyway. The months went by. Then the years. He began to realize something else.

He was never going to be a star. There just weren't enough opportunities.

It was one of his workmates who gave him the great idea.

"Where does it all happen, Freddy boy? Where did Elvis come from — and Frank Sinatra? Where's everybody rich? Where's everything bigger and brighter and better? America, of course! You shouldn't be hanging around here. You oughter go and try your luck on Broadway!"

Once the idea took hold, it wouldn't go away.

A new life in America! A better life for him and Iris! The lights of Broadway! He'd be able to go and hear Frank Sinatra sing whenever he wanted to!

Freddy had a new dream now. One day, somehow, they would go to America.

Then fate took a hand.

'Sunday Night at the London Palladium'

came off the air. The thirty rats were made redundant. The television company was very generous and Mick de Farcey was given a large amount of redundancy money to dispense to his workers, whoever they were.

"Here you are, Freddy. One hundred pounds, less my commission. That's fifty pounds. Didn't I always tell you this job was money for jam?"

Freddy trembled with excitement as he took the bundle of notes.

"Mr de Farcey. How much would it cost me and Iris to get to America? Would this be enough, d'you think? I want to seek a better life, see. For the missus and me."

Mick de Farcey raised his eyebrows. Absent-mindedly he dabbed a little perfume on his mustache, a family habit. He was smiling.

"I'll fix it for you," he said. "Just leave it to me." He held out his hand. "Give us the money back, then."

Freddy complied, then raced back to the sewer to tell Iris the exciting news. But she had some exciting news of her own.

"Guess what, Freddy," she said, as he came through the door. She looked up from her knitting, all pink-cheeked and coy. "There's a little rat on the way."

"Oh blimey, who?" said Freddy. "Not the man from the Council *again.*"

"*Our* own little rat," said Iris, patiently. "We're going to have a baby, Freddy."

The room started to sway around him. All his dreams crashed down about his head.

"I just decided we was going to go to America!" he said.

He sat down on a chair and buried his face in his paws.

"You can't do this to me, Iris," he groaned. "What you want to go and have a baby for? I lost me job today. We're broke. Oh, Iris! We don't want no baby!"

She burst into tears.

And this was the bleak beginning of Roland Rat, superstar and a living legend.

Chapter Seven

THE SINKING OF THE MARRAKECH MAIDEN

"You just go to that pub in Argyle Street and find Mick de Farcey this minute, Freddy Rat," sobbed Iris. "You just go and find him and get that fifty pounds back."

Freddy had told her all about America.

"But Iris, love, I've been thinking. Why can't we still go to America? We want a better life, don't we? And now —" a big lump welled up into his throat " — now you're expecting. Well, we want a better life for our baby, don't we?"

"I don't want to leave London!" Iris wailed. "I'm London born and bred. I want my baby to be born in London! I don't want to leave my nice little home —"

"Nice little 'ome! Come off it, Iris. After all the things you've said about it. . . ."

"But it's home. And we need that fifty pounds for the baby's cot, Freddy. I want to have my baby in hospital and I want to buy a cot. I want our baby to have the best little blankets and pram and high chair in the whole of the sewer —"

"And what will we live on, Iris? I've lost me job. Don't you see, this is me big chance? Broadway! Don't you want me to be a star on Broadway?"

" 'Course I do, Freddy."

She broke into fresh sobs. Freddy couldn't stand it any longer. He came and put an arm round her. For the first time he noticed how big her tummy was.

"All right, all right, love. I'll go and get the fifty pounds back to buy the baby's cot."

"No, Freddy. I'm being selfish! I'd never forgive myself if we didn't go to America. This is your big chance."

She went off to wash her face and powder her nose. When she came back, Freddy had gone.

As he loved Iris so much he had decided to get his redundancy money back from Mick de Farcey, to pay for the baby's cot.

But he was too late.

"It's all fixed, Freddy boy!" Mick de Farcey told him, thrusting two pieces of card into

Freddy's hand. "I've paid over the money and there's your ship. I was just coming to find you. She sails tonight. You've got three hours!"

"But this is a map of Tilbury Docks," said Freddy, peering closely at the top card. "With a cross on it."

"Two maps, as a matter of fact," said Mick. "One for you and one for Iris, in case you lose each other amongst all those cranes and stuff. That cross marks the place where your ship's berthed. She's called the *Marrakech Maiden*."

Freddy began to feel excited.

"That sounds like a posh ship! And she's definitely going to America?"

"Definitely," Mick nodded. "Lovely cruise liner she is. Five star restaurant, swimming pool, ballroom — the lot. You and Iris'll be able to have your second honeymoon. But you'd better get a move on, Freddy boy. Three hours!"

They didn't even have time to pack.

They went and found Freddy's great-uncle and gave him the key to their sewer.

"Make sure nobody goes in there. Don't let nobody touch me things," said Freddy. "Especially not Cliff Richard's comb and Frank Sinatra's carpet. When I've made me name and earned a fortune on Broadway, I'll send you instructions," he said grandly. "I'll want it all put in a trunk and sent out to the States by ship. As soon as we're settled. After that, you can let the sewer to somebody else. But wait till you hear from us."

Iris cried when they said goodbye to the King's Cross sewer. She cried again when they

Star dressing. It's the sophisticated showbiz look for Roland.

The Ratmobile parked outside the secret entrance to the Ratcave at King's Cross.

Roland, in one of his more sensitive roles, as Hamlet. Note particularly the Hamlet costume of string vest and velvet cape.

Little Reggie in his cot with his collection of Roland memorabilia.

Roland was an enormous success when he visited Australia. This is one of his favourite photographs — The Sydney Opera House, which Roland mistook for the Thames Barrier, is in the background.

ERIC THE EAGLE – REGGIE'S FAVOURITE BUT FEROCIOUS PET – WHO RESIDES IN THE THIRD CUBICLE OF THE GENTS TOILET IN THE RATCAVE.

COLIN, ROLAND'S PET FLEA, PERCHED ON HIS FAVOURITE CACTUS IN THE RATCAVE GARDEN.

FERGIE, THE HIGHLAND FERRET, INTERIOR DECORATOR AND ALL-ROUND HANDYMAN, NURSING YET ANOTHER BRUISED FINGER.

DARCEY DE FARCEY, HANDSOME, DEBONAIR, HONEST TO THE CORE AND HEAD OF BBC LIGHT ENTERTAINMENT.

Iris and Freddy, Roland's parents, in a rare romantic mood.

Portrait of Roland's grandfather, Victor — thought to be painted by Piccasso or possibly Handel.

The wedding that never was!
Roland and Glen at the Chapel of the Holy Mackerel deep below King's Cross, before Glenis ran off with Gary Glitter, who Roland had bribed to get her out of his fur!

ERROL *looking boring* IN HONG KONG.

GLENIS, SOON AFTER BEING RESCUED FROM HARRODS' PET DEPARTMENT, IN ONE OF HER FAVOURITE LAURA ASHLEY OUTFITS.

KEVIN AND HIS PINK BUCKET ON THE BEACH AT MINEHEAD.

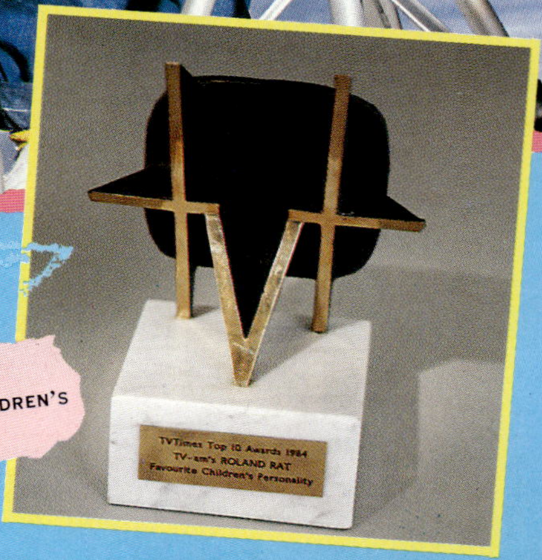

One of Roland's many awards – the TV Times award for Top Children's Personality in 1984.

went and said goodbye to Victor and Winnie, under the London Palladium.

Then it was rush, rush, rush.

Luckily there was a van parked in nearby Carnaby Street, on its way to Tilbury Docks. A consignment of Beatle suits was being shipped to Hamburg. They jumped on the back just before it sped away.

By the time they got to Tilbury it was dark, and Iris was exhausted. But there in the darkness was the huge bulk of the *Marrakech Maiden* ready to sail. They scrambled aboard with two minutes to spare.

They stood on the deck together and watched the twinkling lights of Tilbury recede behind them. The moon came out and danced on the grey waters of the Thames estuary. To sea! To sea!

"America, here we come," said Freddy. "The land of opportunity."

Even Iris was excited now.

"Oh, Freddy, this is our honeymoon, isn't it? Our second honeymoon *and* our first honeymoon."

"I always promised you we'd have a honeymoon, didn't I, Iris?"

"Yes, Freddy. And Freddy —"

"What?"

"Can we have a magical evening together? The first evening of our honeymoon? Can we stroll along the deck in the moonlight, arm in arm?"

" 'Course we can, Iris."

So they started to walk along the deck.

They walked and they walked and they walked.

The cruise liner appeared to consist of one *huge* expanse of flat deck, which seemed to go on for ever and ever.

"I can't see any people, Freddy. Where are all the other passengers — where do you think they are?"

"Dunno," shrugged Freddy. He was daydreaming about arriving in New York. The lights of Broadway! Going to hear Frank Sinatra sing every night! *I did it my way*. He, Freddy Rat, was doing it his way. He'd be a star yet. A great star. A superstar!

The Great American Dream.

"They must be somewhere, Freddy."

"Uh? Oh, I expect they're all down below, love. In the restaurant. Or in the ballroom, dancing the night away. I hope they've got a good band. Mantovani would be nice."

"I can't see any swimming pool, Freddy. There's just this great big deck and nothing else up here."

"It must be down below, Iris."

"I want our cabin, Freedy. Where is it?"

Suddenly Iris was very, very tired and could walk no longer. It was long past their bedtime. Freddy found a piece of tarpaulin covering a pile of planks on deck. They crawled underneath it and snuggled down next to the planks for the night.

"Tomorrow we'll go to the five star restaurant and the ballroom. We'll make this a honeymoon we'll never forget, Iris."

"I'm glad you've brought your bow-tie, Freddy. Freddy —"

"WHAT?"

"Can we go to the heated indoor swimming pool before breakfast? Can we have a swim before breakfast?"

" 'Course we can. But don't you do anything silly like diving off the top board. Not in your condition. Just a nice, gentle swim. Okay?"

Iris's reply was a loud snore. She was sound asleep. It would have been an exhausting day for anyone. For a little lady rat soon to have her baby, it had all been too much.

Next morning the sound of a foghorn woke them up.

The honeymoon couple got up. They were somewhere out at sea. A thick blanket of fog had descended overnight, completely cocooning the *Marrakech Maiden*. The deck was damp and dark and slippery with mist and sea spray. Also it smelt of oil. The boat seemed to be heaving up and down quite alarmingly.

"*Ooh,*" said Iris, hanging on to Freddy for support, as they slowly edged their way along the deck. "I've never seen such a fog, Freddy. You can't see your nose in front of your face."

The mournful sound of the foghorn blasted out again, much louder, much nearer. It was a chilling, ghostly sound.

Freddy peered over the deck rail into the impenetrable fog.

"I hope nothing ain't going to hit us," he said.

Iris slithered as the ship pitched and rolled. She clung on to Freddy, feeling upset and disappointed.

"I thought we'd see rows and rows of tanned people when we woke up this morning," she said. "All sunbathing and relaxing on this great big sun deck. And sipping gins and tonics. But it's all quiet, Freddy, like a ghost ship. It gives me the creeps."

"Don't be daft, Iris. It's only March! Just because this is a luxury cruise liner, it don't mean the passengers are going to come up and sunbathe in the fog. I expect they're all enjoying themselves down below, in the heated indoor swimming pool."

"Let's have our swim before breakfast then," said Iris, brightening up. "You promised. Come on, what we waiting for?"

They groped around in the fog until they found an open hatch. Freddy helped his wife down a long metal ladder. It was secured to the side of a huge steel container. It led down into the bowels of the ship. Gingerly they descended into the pitch black. But they could hear water swishing around at the bottom!

"Listen to that slurping noise!" said Freddy triumphantly. "We've found the swimming pool first go. Only they ain't put the lights on yet. It's not open yet."

"Let's have a swim, my love!" said Iris, in excitement. They lowered themselves into the water.

"Cor!" winced Freddy. "It ain't half cold."

Iris floated on her back for a while, giggling. But when she turned over she got a mouthful of water. She spat it out.

"It's all salty," she said.

There was a sudden juddering crash as

something hit the side of the ship.

"The swimming pool's getting deeper!" exclaimed Iris in alarm.

And deeper and deeper and deeper.

"Quick," said Freddy. "Up the ladder. Let's get back to the deck."

He helped Iris on to the ladder and gave her bottom a push. "Get a move on, love. I'm right behind you."

Puffing and panting they scrambled up the metal rungs, the water swirling up beneath their feet. They were only just keeping ahead of it. Suddenly a crack appeared in the steel wall to which the ladder was fixed. A thick, black sticky liquid spurted out. The liquid had a pungent smell.

"It's oil, Freddy!" wailed Iris. "I've got some on me paws!"

She scrambled on to the deck, Freddy just behind her.

The sea water came swirling up through the open hatch behind them. It gushed across the deck. Some of it looked distinctly oily now.

"The ship's going down!" screamed Iris. "It's sinking!"

"Don't panic, love, I'll save you," said Freddy. Bravely he picked Iris up in his arms and struggled across the deck, knee-deep in angry water. "Them planks that was tied up under that tarpaulin. Quick, here's one. It's come loose!"

A plank was bobbing about on the swirling water, with a length of cord still attached. Freddy pushed Iris down on to the plank, held it steady with his knee, then wrapped the cord round and round both her and the plank.

"Just you lie still. I've tied you on tight so you won't come off. You'll be safe with your Freddy. Don't cry, love."

"Oh, Freddy, our baby. Think of our baby."

With a last sickening lurch and then a violent heave, the *Marrakech Maiden* rolled over and sank.

Thirty seconds later a plank of wood bobbed to the surface of the oily sea. A little figure was securely tied to it, lying on her back, her rather big tummy stuck up in the air. The plank was being towed by another figure, cord between his teeth, swimming valiantly.

The Rats had left the sinking ship.

Chapter Eight

A STAR IS BORN

Somehow Freddy Rat managed to keep ahead of the sinister black slime that followed them. If they got caught in the oil slick, all would be lost. At last he left it behind.

For days and nights Freddy fought his way through the angry seas, towing his precious cargo behind him, the tow-cord gripped tightly between his teeth.

"You all right, Iris?"

"I'm all right, Freddy."

Sometimes it was foggy, sometimes it was clear. All they could ever see was sea, whichever way they looked. Sea and sky, a great overarching sky. At times, when the sea became calm, Freddy would climb up on to the plank beside Iris and tie himself on, too. Then he would snatch some desperately-needed sleep, as they bobbed about on the great blue ocean.

"Those dirty de Farceys," he would say. "I should have listened to Dad. He warned me never to have nothing to do with any de Farcey."

For as they had swum away from that oil slick, the dreadful truth had dawned upon them. The *Marrakech Maiden* was no luxury cruise liner. It had been nothing more than a broken-down old oil tanker, being towed to some distant breaker's yard, perhaps. It had taken only the smallest collision to sink it instantly.

Sometimes Iris would shed a tear.

"It was supposed to be our honeymoon. Rotten cheat. We could have bought the baby's cot with that money."

"But we're *still* going to get to America, Iris," gritted Freddy.

He swam and he swam and he swam, with incredible determination. One single, burning desire gave him super-rat strength. To get to America! To see the lights of Broadway! To seek a better life in the USA! A land of golden opportunity for him — and the chance of a better life for Iris and the baby.

"Will we get there soon, Freddy?" asked Iris

on the fourth day. "You promised I could have my baby in hospital.

" 'Course we will, Iris. And you *will* have the baby in hospital. A big, whacking, shining American hospital with an elevator!"

Secretly he shuddered at the thought of their baby being born at sea, on a bobbing plank in the middle of the inhospitable ocean. He didn't know anything about babies. He didn't even know how they were born. Victor and Winnie had never told him. He *must* get to America.

On the evening of the fifth day they sighted land.

"America!" cried Freddy.

"Oh, Freddy!" wept Iris, in relief. She was weak with hunger and exhaustion. They both were.

Through the gathering dusk they could see the lights of land. Freddy gripped the cord tighter in his teeth, swam faster, his strength almost giving out. Now the shapes of buildings were silhouetted on the skyline.

"The Manhattan skyline," gulped Freddy, in wonder. "Look at all the lights, Iris!"

Nearer. Nearer.

"Look!" Freddy shouted suddenly, swallowing a mouthful of sea in his excitement.

They had just topped a huge wave and he caught a glimpse of a figure. The figure appeared to be standing on a tall platform in the middle of the sea, one arm majestically upraised.

"The Statue of Liberty, Iris!" he cried.

"Where, Freddy? Where?" Strapped to the plank and lying on her back, Iris tried to crane her neck, but they had dipped down into a trough again. And night was falling fast. "I can't see anything, Freddy."

But Freddy saved his breath. He needed every scrap of energy to reach the famous Statue of Liberty. If only he could get there — and rest. Then a passing boat might pick them up and take them in to shore.

As darkness fell he struggled feebly in the direction of the famous landmark. As they topped another wave he saw the figure once again, motionless, silhouetted in the darkness. It was only a few metres ahead of them now. So it wasn't a mirage. It was real . . .

Then something amazing happened.

High above his head, the Statue of Liberty appeared to move, to bend down. It seemed to be throwing a line to them.

The next moment he found himself being lifted bodily out of the sea, a large hook embedded in the seat of his trousers. Then — SPPLITT. There was a tearing sound as the hook ripped away, taking the seat of his pants with it. CRASH! He landed on the high platform flat on his back, the cord connecting him to Iris still gripped tightly in his teeth.

There was a horrible wrenching feeling as though his teeth were being pulled out. He was being dragged along bodily . . . Iris on her plank was now dangling over the side! He grabbed the cord in both hands, got to his feet, and began to heave.

One, two, three . . .

As the plank slithered over the edge of the platform, with Iris still safely on board, Freddy nearly fainted with relief.

"What's happening, Freddy?" she gasped.

"It's all right, love." He ran over, untied her, then helped her to her feet. "It's all right. We're safe. We're safe."

"How did we get up here, Freddy?"

"It was the Statue of Liberty. It saved us."

"Rubbish. How can a statue move?"

The statue was bending over them, even now. Was it hallucination after all those days at sea? No — it was real.

A feeling of elation swept through Freddy. Peering up through the darkness, he reached up a small paw.

"Shake, kid!" he said boisterously. "Guess you'd like to know who I am, eh? I'm Freddy Rat and this is Iris and we're from the old country. It sure is great to meet a famous statue like you. Gee whizz, what a great welcome to little old New York."

The figure appeared not to hear them.

It walked away into the gloom and shouted to someone, "Oi, Alfie. Come and see what we got here. A couple o' drowned rats. Just broken me flamin' fishing line, they have. Let's bang 'em on the head!"

But when Alfie came over, Freddy and Iris were nowhere to be seen.

They were running, as fast as their legs would carry them.

The entire length of Southend Pier.

In the guard's van of a train back to London, they found warmth, shelter — and food. There was a huge carton of crisps in transit. Freddy opened it, found their favourite flavours. Then they worked their way through four whole packets. They washed that down with a bottle of bitter lemon.

"So we never got to America, after all," said Freddy, dully.

"Mmmm. Cheese and onion and bitter lemon!" said Iris cheerfully. "My favourites. I never been so hungry in all my life, Freddy."

"The end of my dreams," he said. "I'll never be a star now. We're a doomed family, Iris. It's our feud with them wicked, grasping de Farceys. It goes on from generation to generation."

"Oh, shut up moaning, Freddy. You've been reading too many books. We're alive, aren't we?" She snuggled up to him. "We're all right. Me and the baby. We could have died. That's what matters isn't it? And you know something, Freddy? You're my hero. You deserve a medal."

She snuggled up to him, warm in the rattling train, and kissed him.

Freddy began to feel more cheerful.

When they got off the train at Liverpool Street station there were tears of joy in Iris's eyes.

"London!" she whispered. "Home!"

After all, she'd never wanted to go to America in the first place.

As they threaded their way across Liverpool Street station, arm in arm, Iris suddenly gripped Freddy very tightly.

"What's the matter, Iris?"

"It's the baby, Freddy. The baby's coming."

"Let's get back to King's Cross quick then,"

said Freddy, in alarm. "Back home to our own little sewer. I'll call the midwife . . ."

"I want to have my baby in hospital!" wailed Iris. "I want to go to hospital in a taxi like my cousin did. You promised me, Freddy."

"Aw, all right then."

There was a cab rank outside the station. The first taxicab in the queue was just beginning to move off. Freddy tugged his wife's hand.

"Quick!"

They scrambled up on to the rear bumper. Then they clung on for dear life as it jolted through the London streets.

A great feeling of joy flooded through Iris. She was going by taxi to have her baby in hospital!

The taxi pulled up at some traffic lights, right beside one of London's most classy maternity hospitals. Freddy and Iris jumped off.

They scampered in through a side entrance and found a friendly mouse clearing up some crumbs in the corridor.

The mouse sized up the situation at a glance.

"First floor, third door on the left," she said. "That's the Rodent Maternity Wing."

They found it and Iris was admitted.

It was a spacious broom cupboard. Several other rats were bedded down, waiting to have their babies. There were unlimited supplies of free milk powder, if required, in the kitchen next door. An ante-room full of medicines was just across the corridor, in case of complications. Rodents' Maternity was very handily placed.

"Oh, Freddy, it's lovely," breathed Iris, as he made her comfortable on a pile of dusters. Her time had come. "Leave me alone, love. I'm going to have the baby very soon."

"She'll be all right," said the acting midwife. "You just go and wait in the corridor."

Freddy shot outside in relief. But he couldn't stand still. He was in a state of great agitation and excitement. He paced up and down, paws clasped behind his back as he was very embarrassed about his torn pants.

A few moments before the birth something truly amazing happened.

Through the window at the end of the corridor, Freddy saw sheet lightning illuminate the London sky, turning the clouds silver — then purple — then black!

He trembled as there followed roll upon roll of thunder.

On West End theatres, the names of the famous stars emblazoned in lights dipped several times as though in silent homage.

TV sets flickered as far afield as Basingstoke and Milton Keynes.

It was exactly ten o'clock at night.

These were portents — great portents. Portents of Shakespearean magnitude.

Then the heavens opened and the rains fell with the force of Niagara. There was a flash flood, the like of which London had never seen before.

Water cascaded down the streets in swirling torrents. Drains overflowed and manhole covers lifted.

All the sewers flooded.

Then, silence. The dramatic storm ended as suddenly as it had begun.

The door of the broom cupboard opened and the acting midwife peeped out. She beckoned to Freddy.

In a low, awe-struck voice, she said:

"Your baby arrived at ten o'clock. It's a boy. A lovely little boy rat. The loveliest baby in the ward."

Thus was announced:

THE

BIRTH

OF

ROLAND

RAT

The proud father walked in and held his little son in his arms.

He and Iris gazed at each other, misty-eyed.

All the heartbreak, the anguish, the physical suffering of the past few days was forgotten. Freddy walked tall.

"Can we call him Pisces?" suggested Iris. "It's the twelfth of March."

"Don't be daft!" said Freddy.

They argued and bickered. Finally they decided on *Roland*, after Freddy's great-great-grandfather.

"Roll for short," said Iris.

The next day they took their baby son home to the King's Cross sewer. It was only just beginning to dry out after the flood. Freddy laid baby Roland gently on Frank Sinatra's carpet for a few moments and gazed at him with great emotion.

In their courting days, he and Iris had seen *Gone With The Wind* six times and now Vivien Leigh's immortal words came back to him. He said — "As Frank Sinatra is my witness . . . As Frank Sinatra is my witness . . . I will never go hungry again."

"How do you work that out, Freddy?" asked Iris.

Freddy knew that his own dreams of stardom had vanished for ever. But slowly, haltingly, he declared:

"Our Roll is going to be a star one day. De Farceys or no de Farceys, our Roll is going to be a star."

Chapter Nine

ROLAND'S EARLY STRUGGLES

The proud parents, from a very early stage, started to look out eagerly for any sign of talent in their baby son.

"Freddy, Freddy, come and look!" Iris exclaimed one day. Roland was just a few months old. "Come and look at what his little legs are doing."

Roland was lying on his back, kicking. On the transistor radio, David Jacobs had just put on a record of Elvis Presley singing *Love Me Tender . . .*

"What, Iris?"

"Look, his little legs are kicking in time to the music."

When Roland was a year old — more excitement!

He was in his high chair being naughty with his baby dinner. Iris was sitting knitting Roland some little blue leggings and waiting for Freddy to come home from work.

Freddy was a humble scavenger in the kitchens of the Trocadero these days. He worked split duty and sometimes came home for lunch.

On this particular day he marched in singing a Beatles hit that he had been whistling all morning.

She loves me . . . Yeah! Yeah! Yeah!

She loves me . . . Yeah! Yeah! Yeah!

Suddenly Roland threw his little spoon on the floor and croaked:

"YEAH"

And then —

"YEAH . . . YEAH!"

Iris and Freddy hugged each other, speechless with excitement.

"Hear that, Iris?" said Freddy, finding his voice at last. "I didn't dream it, did I?"

"No, Freddy."

"Our little Roll. Singing. Just like his Dad," said Freddy proudly. "And he's only just one. Ordinary little rats when they first open their mouths just say stupid things like *Mumma* and *Dudda*. But not our Roll. He opens his mouth and sings a famous hit song!"

"YEAH . . . YEAH," repeated Roland. "YEAH!"

It was a cracked and tuneless sound to ordinary ears. But to Freddy and Iris it was liquid beauty . . . Frank Sinatra, Cliff Richard, Maria Callas and Elvis Presley, all rolled into one.

"We're a showbiz family, Roll," his father used to tell him. "And don't you ever forget it."

There was no danger of poor Roland forgetting it.

Throughout his childhood, all his father ever talked to him about was show business! Especially his memories.

After working hard all week, clearing the floor at the Trocadero, there was nothing Freddy liked better than to relax at home on a Sunday afternoon, smoking a pipe and reminiscing.

His young son, sitting at his feet, heard the same stories over and over again.

What it had been like to be born under a dressing room at the London Palladium. The glamour — the glitter — the smell of greasepaint!

"Can't I go and smell, Dad?" Roland asked him once. He was hoping to cut his father short, so that he could get on with playing with his Action Man for a change. "If you let me go and smell I'd know all about it then."

" 'Course not, son," his father said irritably.

The dressing rooms had been modernised three years earlier. Victor and Winnie had been made homeless. They were now living in a little hovel, just along the sewer.

"The old homestead's been destroyed, Roll," said Freddy. "Progress, that's what they call it. Why d'you think your grandparents had to move back to King's Cross? Besides," he added, "you smell already. Ho! Ho!"

On . . . and on . . . and on.

What it had been like getting his big chance in showbiz.

Working in TV. One of the regulars on 'Sunday Night at the London Palladium'. The revolving stage, the bright lights, the romance, all the rats he worked with calling each other "darling". All of them dreaming of the big breakthrough. Of being called up on to that stage by Bruce Forsyth . . .

The passage of time softens most things and it had certainly softened Freddy's brain! He looked back on those years through rose-tinted spectacles, forgetting all the hard grind and the heartbreak, remembering only the good times and the glamour.

Then on a Sunday evening, more often than not, a gaggle of giggling girl mice would come knocking at the door, asking Freddy to sing to them.

He would entertain them with all the Cliff Richard hits. Always Cliff Richard, till quite late in the evening —

We're all going on a Summer Holiday . . .
— and from his bedroom Roland would hear his mother's voice, peeved, querulous:

"Come on, Freddy. Enough's enough. You'll wake up little Roll. Just tell those girls it's time they went home."

Most boring of all, by Roland's standards,

were those weekends when Freddy had spent too long at the pub. He would come home, maudlin and depressed. Taking his young son by the hand, he would tell him about the wicked, perfumed-mustachioed de Farceys. Then after giving his nose a good blow, he would run through his entire collection of showbiz memorabilia, item by item.

The collection was getting very tired and tatty looking.

The moths had got at Johnny Ray's handkerchief. Tommy Steele's coke bottle had mildew growing on the inside. Frank Sinatra's carpet was completely threadbare. And all the old theatre programmes were brown, faded and curling at the edges.

Freddy would lovingly finger each programme and pass it over to his son to examine. Then, every so often, he would launch into a long story about a particular star or a particular show.

Soon Roland knew all the stories off by heart. And being a normal, boisterous little male rat he would have preferred to be out in the sewer with the other lads, picking a fight, or up on the tube platforms doing some train spotting.

It was only at the end of these sessions that Roland would brighten up slightly.

His father always ended with the same speech, give or take a word or two.

"Roll, when you're a bit older I want you to go out there into that big world of humans. Your granddad and I never really had the guts, but you, Roll, you can do it. Prove to the rodent world that you're just as good as Elvis or Frank Sinatra. Prove to them that Roland Rat Rules OK!"

Roland was too young to understand fully what his Dad was on about. But he liked the sound of that last bit. Roland Rat Rules OK. Yeah. He liked the sound of that.

Freddy was the dreamer. Iris was a bit more practical.

"Roll's never going to be a star like this. Talk, talk, talk! That's never going to turn our boy into a star, Freddy Rat. I want our Roll to go to dancing classes!"

"Dancing classes?"

"Miss Bittle's School of Dance and Drama. It's only just up the road at the Angel. The human kids learn tap-dancing there. And deportment — and music and movement! Look at the way the big stars handle their bodies — Elvis, Marilyn Monroe. They start young, that's what. They learn how to project themselves."

"How d'you know about this place then?"

"I've seen the adverts in the *Evening Standard*."

"I've never had no dancing. I never had no deportment classes."

"And look where it got you," said Iris.

"What's it going to cost?" asked Freddy.

"No more than you spend on beer, Freddy Rat. If you gave up your pints and I took in some more sewing, we could manage it."

Freddy's jaw sagged.

"Do you want our Roll to be a failure like you, or do you want him to be a star?"

"I want him to be a star, don't I," said Freddy stoutly.

So it was all settled.

Iris got busy with her sewing machine. She made Roland some tight-fitting blue velvet trousers, a white frilly shirt and a cummerbund. They couldn't afford to buy him any tap shoes so Freddy hammered some old bits of tin on to the heels and toes of Roland's everyday boots.

At the start of the new term, they pushed Roland off to Miss Bittle's School of Dance and Drama.

" 'Bye, Roll," said Iris, a little tear in her eye.

"Got your money, son?" said Freddy. "You go do us proud. Get over there and show Miss Bittle how much talent you got! Remember you come from a showbiz family, son, and you're going to be a star."

Now he'd got used to it, Freddy was really excited. In fact he claimed that the whole idea had been his.

Roland slunk along the sewer in shame. He kept into the wall, sneaking along sideways, darting from shadow to shadow.

He was scared lest any of his mates saw him in the blue velvet pants and frilly shirt. He could hear their voices echoing in the sewer, shouting raucously as they played football.

He knew a run up to the Northern line, platform 3. When he got to it, he dived into it in relief. It was the very same run that his grandfather Victor had used in those far-off days when he'd gone up top to collect whelks.

By the time Roland reached Miss Bittle's at the Angel, he was quaking with nerves. He also felt a bit stupid. He could hear a piano tinkling inside and a plummy voice saying:

"One . . . two . . . three . . . stretch. Sharon, you're not STRE-T-T-CHING. Come along, Wayne. Remember you're a little flower, reaching up TOWARDS THE SUN . . . NO, YOU CAN'T be a caterpillar . . . One . . . two . . . three . . ."

"Roland Rat Rules OK," he muttered to give himself courage. Then he walked straight in and joined on the end of a line of children. He started stretching in time to the music.

He heard his pants spilt and went hot with embarrassment.

"Now — deportment. Each of you take a book from the pile," said Miss Bittle. "I want you to walk round and round the room, in time to the music, with the book balanced on your head. No hands. I want you all to walk like straight little soldiers."

To the tinkling rhythm of "The Grand Old Duke of York", they lined up with books on heads, Roland at the end.

But he had scarcely taken four steps when his book fell to the floor with a loud thud. It fell on Sharon's toe and she wailed loudly.

Miss Bittle ceased playing the piano, swung round and surveyed the class. She peered short-sightedly through her spectacles at Roland.

"You — the little one at the end. Come over here."

In an agony of embarrassment, Roland shuffled across to her. He was scared that his pants might split some more.

"Your posture is terrible," she said.

Roland hung his head.

"Your attempts to be a flower just now were *pathetic.*"

Roland began to feel more cheerful.

"You have no talent. No charisma. No presence whatsoever . . ."

She peered at him more closely.

"Can you tell me Mum and Dad that?" Roland was asking eagerly.

'What's more," shrilled Miss Bittle in disgust: "You're a *rat* and you stink!"

"Don't you want me money, miss?"

"Get out!" she screeched. "Get out!"

Roland ran for it.

Once he was out in the street, he rolled over and over in the gutter in joy. Lovely mud! No more blue velvet pantaloons. No more dancing lessons!

He kicked a stone all the way home, whistling cheerfully. This would shut Dad up, good and proper. And Mum!

And it did.

For quite a while.

Roland's early struggles against his destiny were only to be expected.

But destiny was going to win in the end.

Chapter Ten

AN OXBRIDGE REJECT

As the years went by, out of sheer idle-mindedness, Roland began to accept the inevitable. Freddy told him so frequently that he was going to be a star that by the time he was in his teens, Roland believed it himself.

"Give me a hand with the dishes, Roll," Iris would say to her teenage son. "Get your feet off the kitchen table and give me a hand."

But Roland would sit there, slurping down

cups of coffee, wiping his mouth on the back of his denim sleeve and crudely strumming tunelessly on his guitar.

"Shurrup, mum, I'm practising me new number. You know I'm fantastic, mum. You know I'm going to be a star."

"I hope you make plenty of money then," Iris would grumble. "I'm fed up with living in this place! The walls are so thin you can hear the neighbours talking. The roof's leaking! And all the furniture's falling to pieces."

Baby Reggie had arrived by now (a very windy baby) and there was another mouth to feed.

Iris would paw over her favourite magazines. She was always hunting through dustbins and dragging them back to the sewer. She loved *Homes and Gardens*. She used to think wistfully of her comfortable childhood in Euston.

"Your father's never done anything with his life," she would grumble. "Look at this, Roll. I want a house like this. Look at the lovely decor, all those beautiful chintz fabrics. *Mmmm*. Sliding doors on to the patio! Roll, isn't it lovely."

"You wait till I'm a star, Mum. I'll build a fantastic place down here. You and Dad and little Reggie will have your own apartment with three jacuzzis and two saunas an' . . ."

"What do we want all those for, Roll?"

"I dunno, Mum."

Then Freddy would come home, moaning about his job and the way the price of beer was going up.

It was a depressing atmosphere for a sensitive, artistic, talented young rat to grow up in.

So one day when his father came home from work, Roland's ears pricked up with interest.

"Our Roll needs a good education, that's what," he heard him say to Iris.

"What? You mean go to school?"

"School!" scoffed Freddy. "School? Don't be daft. You know what them places are like. All over the papers they are. I don't hold with 'em. Fighting, hitting their teachers, scrawling graffiti on the walls. You don't think I'd let our Roll go to a place like that?"

"Well what you talking about then? He tried for the Royal Academy of Dramatic Art, didn't he, and they wouldn't have him because he was a rat."

Freddy paced up and down the kitchen, looking pleased with himself.

"Stars are cultured nowadays. They're posh. They've been educated. It's not what you know, it's who you know."

"I don't follow you," said Iris, with some justification.

"Our Roll's not going to grow up into some moronic slob. Before he starts being a famous star he's got to go to university! *University*. Roland Rat, B.A. (Hons)."

"How?"

"Lend me a fiver from the housekeeping, Iris. You'll soon find out."

Freddy had met the pleasant young man with the mustache at lunch-time. They'd found themselves sharing a bench in the Embankment Gardens, both enjoying the sunshine. He wasn't at all stand-offish, like most humans, and

Freddy soon found himself boasting about his son Roland.

"What I'd really like is for my Roll to go to university," he'd confided. "I got this handbook from a place called UCCA. But not being educated like, I can't make head nor tail of it, so to speak."

"Oh, I know all about UCCA," said the young fellow, dabbing a touch of perfume on his mustache. "It stands for the Universities' Central Council for Admissions. It's in Cheltenham, and they've got a big computer there. This computer sorts out all the applications. It digests what "A" levels and "O" levels everybody's got and then spews out acceptances for university."

"My Roll ain't got no exams," said Freddy sadly.

"So what? A friend of mine can get him in for you. He's a hacker."

"What? You mean he breaks down doors with an axe?"

"No! He's a computer wizard. Got a couple of fantastic computers. He can hack his way into anybody else's computer programme and make it do what he wants."

"You serious?" asked Freddy, in excitement.

"Never been more so. He hacked into the Buckingham Palace computer last month and rearranged Her Majesty's royal tour. Just for a laugh. Instead of going to Italy she ended up in Siberia. The month before that he hacked into the Star Wars research programme and mixed it up with the Margarine Stock Levels off the Tesco computer. That should be funny. Getting your lad into university will be child's play to a brain like his. Give me a fiver to slip him and it'll be done in a trice."

"Garn!" said Freddy.

So he met up with the man that evening and handed over the five pound note.

"I don't even know your name," he said.

"Just call me Darcey," said the man. He took the fiver, smiled, and gave an ingratiating bow.

"You fool, Freddy Rat," said Iris when her husband got home. "Mick de Farcey had a young nephew called Darcey — don't you remember? You can kiss goodbye to that five pound note. You'll never hear from *him* again."

But Iris was wrong.

Exactly one week later, a stack of letters came in the post.

They were all addressed to Mr Roland Rat. Some were brochures, setting out the delights of various universities. Five were from UCCA headquarters in Cheltenham. Little slips of computer paper, offering Roland an unconditional place at five different universities: London, Edinburgh, Cardiff, Durham — and Oxford.

All Roland had to do was to choose which one to go to, sign the acceptance slip, and post it back to Cheltenham.

"You look lovely, Roll. Just lovely," said Iris. She had made him a little black scholar's gown and a mortar board. He was about to leave King's Cross sewer for Oxford.

"Off you go then, son," said Freddy. "And good luck with the interview." His chest was all swollen up with pride.

"I don't need no luck," said Roland airily, blowing on his fingernails. "They want me pretty bad up there. Didn't you read the letter from the Prof?"

In fact they'd all read the letter several times, before hanging it in a frame above the mantelpiece. It was on heavily-embossed, crested notepaper. It said:

OXFORD From the Emeritus Professor of Philosophy

Dear Mr Rat,

We are delighted to see that you have accepted our unconditional offer of a place here to study Philosophy and Psychology. In view of your outstanding qualifications of 37 "O" levels, 16 "A" levels all at Grade A and three distinctions at "S" level, all the colleges are fighting to have you. I suggest we meet in my rooms for our formal interview (and I stress that this is a mere formality) and you can decide which college you prefer. The food at Merton is excellent as they have their own chef, but you may prefer St. Anne's, where there are more girls.

(SIGNED) Bertie

Girls. Yeah!

Nevertheless, Roland wasn't as calm as he looked. He had feelings beneath that brash exterior. Above all, he was sensitive about being a rat. When he got to Oxford he tried to be as inconspicuous as possible. In his mortar board and black gown he walked down the High, mingling with the other students, his nose buried deep in the Oxford University handbook.

It was full of helpful tips about The Interview. Oxford was not looking for achievement, it said, but for promise. That was a bit of luck, thought Roland. Don't be frightened to argue with the person who interviews you, it said. Oxford was not looking for spongy minds that simply absorbed facts — but for questioning, probing minds! Above all, don't bother about being polite . . . .

Roland liked the sound of that.

He found the ancient college, set in its magnificent gardens by the river. He went up a back staircase, the stone steps worn down by centuries of use. He tapped on the door of the Emeritus Professor.

"Come in, old chap."

Roland found himself in a huge, book-lined study. To one side was a table which held a decanter full of sherry and two sparkling crystal glasses.

The Professor sat with his feet up on a large walnut desk, reading a copy of *The Times*. This was held up in front of his face, so all Roland could see was a pair of tweed-trousered legs sticking out from under the open newspaper.

"Pour yourself a sherry, Roland. Get me one while you're about it."

Roland filled the glasses to the brim and took them over. He climbed on a chair that was set this side of the desk. The Professor's hand came out from behind the newspaper, reached across the desk and took the proferred glass.

"Thanks, old chap."

There was the sound of a glass being drained behind *The Times* and the smacking of lips. Roland followed suit. He was beginning to enjoy this.

"What do you say about Wittgenstein?" the voice suddenly rapped.

"A load of old rubbish," replied Roland.

"Splendid. You Eton?"

"I gotta pork pie and chips on the train," replied Roland.

An appreciative chuckle and the rustle of pages being turned. "Proletariat, eh? Splendid. Don't listen to anybody who tells you Oxford is a bastion of privilege. We're *positively* discriminating these days. Went to a council school, I hope?"

"Didn't go to school at all. Me Dad don't hold wiv 'em."

"Excellent. Now, tell me. Do you think Kant had it right? Is this table where we think it is, or is it just a figment of our imagination?"

"It was you what put the booze out, not me," retorted Roland.

"Quite so! And where does that leave Descartes?"

"In front of de horses, sir! Yeah!!!"

The professor roared with laughter and his newspaper heaved up and down.

"You're in, Roland. I look forward to having you at my tutorials. We'll just find you a college and sign you in."

He lowered his newspaper, swung his legs off the desk and rose to his feet. He peered around the room from beneath a mop of wild, greyish-coloured hair. Finally his eyes focussed on Roland, standing there on the chair in the gown and mortar board.

"My word. You're a rat," he said.

"He really liked me! Mum . . . Dad . . . He said I was great. He'd have liked me at Oxford, honest," explained Roland when he got home. "It was just University Regulations. He said you could move heaven and earth and still not be able to bend 'em. He said it took 'em four hundred years just to let women in."

"That Darcey de Farcey!" said Freddy, darkly. "Taking our money."

"*My* money," sniffed Iris. "My housekeeping money. He never mentioned any regulations when he took my housekeeping money!"

But Roland wasn't downcast. Far from it.

The Oxford episode had given his confidence a great boost. He swanked around the sewer in his mortar board and gown for weeks on end. Hadn't his Dad always told him he was special? He *was* special. He would be a star one day — the greatest star that ever lived!

He started getting up late in the morning. He stopped bothering to wash. Why should he bother? He was the greatest, wasn't he? Brill, ace and skill!

Then finally, one fateful morning, Freddy's patience snapped.

"You smell, Roll!" he said. He threw his newspaper at him in disgust. "In fact you stink! When you going to make something of yourself?"

Roland caught the newspaper and stared at it.
"Here, look at this, Dad," he said.

BREAKFAST TV ARRIVES, said the headline. NEW TALENT NEEDED.

Chapter Eleven

THE INCREDIBLE BREAKTHROUGH

Roland ran out into the sewer, holding tight to the newspaper.

"Where d'you think you're going with my paper?" shouted his father.

"This is it, Dad! My big chance!"

"Bring that paper back, you young tear-away!"

Roland was already halfway along the sewer. He looked back and shouted at Freddy.

"I'm going to be a star, stupid!"

The words echoed and reverberated majestically, up and down the sewer. All the neighbours looked out.

STAR STUPID . . . STUPID . . . STUPID . . . STAR!

Freddy just sighed with relief. "Oh well, that's all right then. I'll buy another paper." He went back inside and shut the front door.

"What was all that about?" asked Iris.

"Our Roll's going to be a star," said Freddy smugly. "Something to do with Breakfast TV. It was in the paper."

As Roland hot-footed it over to the new TV station his heart was going bang-bang, bang-bang.

A new company had started up, making programmes for Breakfast TV. The building was near King's Cross! And they needed talent — they needed it desperately. That's what it said.

According to the story in the newspaper, the whole thing was a frost. People were switching off their TVs all over Britain. It seemed they preferred to watch their eggs and bacon sizzling in the pan, or their cereal going snap, crackle and pop.

There was some indefinable star quality missing . . . .

"Me!" thought Roland. "That's what's missing!"

The world had been waiting for him all this time — and now his moment had come.

He didn't care that he hadn't washed that morning, that he'd rushed out of the sewer in his faded jeans, denim cap and a football sweater. He didn't care!

He reached the imposing modern block. The main doors were made of glass and led into a carpeted reception area. As he approached, the doors slid back electronically as though to say: *Welcome, your majesty. This way, please.*

Beyond, two receptionists sat with their heads bowed in deep concentration, putting purple varnish on their nails and wondering how long their jobs were going to last.

They didn't notice the short figure sweep through the silent doors and march purposefully towards them across the deep pile carpet.

"Coo, what a horrible stink," said the first girl.

"Must be this nail varnish, Trace," replied her friend.

"Tell your boss *I'm 'ere*," said a purposeful voice below the reception desk.

"Name, please?" asked Tracey, without looking up. (Or down).

"Roland Rat."

Mechanically the girl jiggled the telephone switchboard and went through to her boss.

"A Mr Roland Rat to see you, sir."

"What's his business?" crackled a despairing voice.

"What's your business?" she flung back over her shoulder.

Roland told her.

"He says he's an incredibly talented versatile star, sir. He pongs a bit."

Her boss was sitting at his desk in the boardroom with a huge bottle of aspirins in front of him, contemplating suicide.

"I don't care if he reeks," he said eagerly. "Send him straight up."

The two girls watched Roland's back view disappear jauntily into the lift.

"What a funny looking bloke," said Tracey. "He could easily have been a rat."

"So what, Trace? That's show business."

"Come in!" said the big boss eagerly, as Roland tapped on the door.

"*I'm 'ere!*" beamed Roland, as he bounced into the executive suite. He flung his arms wide and jumped up on to a chair. "You want talent, I got talent. Yeah!" He broke into song. "You want rhythm . . . I got rhythm . . . who could ask for anything more? Yeah — yeah! Well, sir —" He made an extravagant bow and held the pose. "Here I am. I've come to save your show. The most brilliant, versatile, highly-talented, one-and-only, amazing —

"OOO-OWWWWW!"

Roland found himself flying out of the room on the end of a boot. He crash-landed in the corridor and the door was slammed on him.

"Revolting!" shouted the big boss through the closed door. "You're nothing more than a common sewer rat. A horrible, smelly rat. Get out of my office! Get out of my building. Times may be bad, but we're not that desperate!"

The boss returned to his desk, hollow-eyed, to contemplate the bottle of aspirins once more.

Roland got up and dusted himself down. That was the moment when the iron entered his soul.

He thought of his family, fighting for fulfilment and recognition for three long generations.

He scowled at the closed door and gritted to himself, "*What a crude man. You can tell he ain't been to Oxford.*"

Roland might be a sensitive artiste underneath, but now he developed a toughness, a real cool exterior. You needed real cool to survive the ups and downs of show business. One look at his pathetic old dad, Freddy, and his broken-down old granddad, Victor, told him that.

Hands in his pockets, he mooched up to the top of the building. Then out on to its flat roof. He walked around the roof and surveyed the whole of London spread before him.

It gave him a great sense of power — of destiny!

All those little streets with their rows of chimneys. And on the chimneys, rows and rows of television aerials. Waiting to receive him. Roland Rat — superstar.

The world was waiting for him! Breakfast TV needed him. Needed his charisma, his hidden and indefinable *star quality*. He'd show 'em.

His Dad's immortal words rang in his brain. *Prove to the rodent world that you're just as good as Elvis or Frank Sinatra. Prove to them that Roland Rat Rules OK!*

Yeah.

And suddenly Roland knew what he was going to do.

He found some planks and a hammer and nails. With all the fervour of the true pioneer, he set about building a shed up there on the roof, with his bare hands. He was going to build his *own* television studio!

Bit by bit, he found all the technology surplus to requirements downstairs and lying around in cupboards. He crept around stealthily and brought it up to his shed on the roof, one piece at a time.

When it was all installed, he got hold of the most important thing of all — a transmitter! He was pleased to see that it was good quality one. He knew he'd have to beam out a powerful signal. So powerful that it would drown out the rubbish they were putting out below.

Yeahhh! Roland laughed to himself. *Big world, here I come.*

Thus it was that in April 1983 came one of the greatest technological triumphs of our age.

The Rodent Broadcasting Corporation went on the air.

Roland's television debut was the sensation of the 1980s. He was an immediate hit — a superstar.

On the morning of the third day the postman staggered up to the rodent's studio on the roof with a whole sackful of fan mail.

It should have arrived the day before, but it had all been posted first class.

When Freddy and Iris viewed Roland's first broadcast, on the little black-and-white TV set at home, with all the neighbours crowding in to watch, Freddy did something he'd wanted to do since he was a teenager.

He went and stood on Frank Sinatra's carpet,

and took something out of his and Iris's bedside table. It was something very precious. He found a match. Then he lit up Elvis Presley's cigarette stub[2] and took a drag.

By the morning of the fifth day the fan mail had increased to eight sackloads and a team of postmen was required to deliver it.

And by the end of the first week, the big boss down below crumpled and caved in. Pressure was being put on him by millions of viewers and, even more important, his shareholders.

He came up to the roof and knocked on the door of the wooden shed, wringing his hands and sobbing.

"Please come and work in our studios downstairs, Mr Rat," he begged. He touched his forelock and produced a contract. "You're wonderful. Wonderful. A great star. I was wrong about you. Please sign here."

What a creeper, thought Roland. *But he's right. I'm a great star.*

So he signed the contract.

After three generations of grinding poverty, the Rat family had finally fulfilled their destiny. At last, through Roland, they had made it. The incredible breakthrough.

[2] *See biographer's note (1) on p. 26. The evidence having been destroyed in this way, it seems that the controversy started by Dr. Lisa Lott cannot be resolved and could well rage forever.*

Chapter Twelve

ROLAND RAT — LIVING LEGEND

The rest is history. Roland Rat is no longer merely a great star. He's a *superstar* — a living legend.

His world has changed, beyond recognition.

From the moment that the Rodent Broadcasting Corporation hit the airwaves, Roland was more than just a smash hit with the humans. He became a symbol to downtrodden rodents everywhere, a rallying-point.

There began to gather round him a charmed circle that represented the best and most vibrant young rodent talents in the world today.

Kevin. The gerbil who travelled down from the north country just to be able to shake his hero's hand — and remained to become Roland's friend, confidant and business manager.

Errol. The charming and sometimes boring hamster from Wales, with his magnificent collection of leeks.

Glenis. The beautiful, upper-class guinea-pig, with the lovely singing voice — who had been languishing in the pets' department at Harrods until she heard about Roland and got him to rescue her.

Fergie. The proudly nationalistic Scot (and ferret) from Glasgow's Gorbals: bagpiper and interior decorator extraordinary.

And Colin, the singing flea. Roland's most private admirer, whose close assocations with the rodent world gave him an entrée.

Last but not least there's little Reggie, Roland's own small brother . . . a very special talent.

In 1984, two spectacular *Rat on the Road* shows brought out capacity crowds the length and breadth of Britain, enabling Roland to meet some of his myriad fans. There followed overseas tours, and then more TV appearances.

And finally — the inevitable.

As the British Broadcasting Corporation watched their ratings slump to zero, they poached Roland from their rivals. They made him an offer he couldn't refuse. The chance to open a new TV channel, his very own.

BBC 3, starring Roland Rat, opened in 1986.

With fame came all the trappings of money and success. Unfortunately he is still lumbered with his 1953 Ford Anglia sprayed pink otherwise known as the Ratmobile. But the jewel in Roland's crown is undoubtedly his architect-designed home.

The Ratcave lies deep in the main sewer below King's Cross station. Descent is via a hydraulically-operated parking bay inside a workman's hut, activated by a special rodent I.D. card in the parking meter outside. Once down below, entry to the inner sanctum is by a password which is changed daily.

The Ratcave, labyrinthine in its complexity, is talked about by rodents the world over — from California to Katmandu.

In the sub-basement there's a beautiful underground marina; above that a recreation area, complete with rose garden and swings for Little Reggie. The four levels above that house the five wonders of the underground world: Roland's personal recording studios, discotheque, solarium, gymnasium and cocktail bar.

Apart from Roland's own magnificent suite, there are spare rooms for all members of his circle (including a boudoir for Glenis, which Iris sometimes uses but not often) and a beautifully appointed apartment for his mum and dad and Little Reggie. In fact Iris is allowed to change the furnishings and curtains every three months if she wants to.

The whole lot is topped off on Level 1 with an underground garage for the Ratmobile, complete with service bay, plus a hangar for Roland's private aircraft. Kevin is in charge of that and runs a little business called Kev-Air on the side.

Roland Rat has come a long way since the days when he was a scruffy urchin, listening to his father's reminiscences in the King's Cross sewer when it used to be a slum.

He is, indeed, a rodent of substance.

As he lolls in lavish luxury it might be easy to imagine that success could spoil him, could make him big-headed. But no.

"Our Roll's just the same as he's always been," vows Iris. "Modest to a fault."

"Hasn't changed a bit," agrees Freddy. "We're a fulfilled family now, us Rats. Thanks to our Roll. I always said he could do it!"

Of course, there's just one small cloud on the horizon.

As the authorized life story has exclusively revealed — where there's money to be made, there will you find a de Farcey.

Within a week of Roland making his name in showbiz, Darcey de Farcey came back into their lives.

And there he remains to this day. There's just no shaking him off. Which only goes to prove that every silver lining has a cloud and even living legends have their problems.

But each time Darcey de Farcey appears on the big colour TV at Hendon, Roland's granddad, dear old Victor, switches the sound off and shouts abuse at the screen.

Victor remembers Anton de Farcey, in those far-distant days, the dark days of the London Blitz, and it gives him great pleasure to have the last word.